Cuyahoga Valley National Park

by Joanne Mattern

Content Consultant

Nanci R. Vargus, Ed.D.
Professor Emeritus, University of Indianapolis

Reading Consultant

Jeanne M. Clidas, Ph.D.
Reading Specialist

Children's Press®

An Imprint of Scholastic Inc.

Library of Congress Cataloging-in-Publication Data

Names: Mattern, Joanne, 1963- author.
Title: Cuyahoga Valley National Park/by Joanne Mattern.
Description: New York, NY: Children's Press, an imprint of Scholastic Inc., [2019] | Series: Rookie national parks | Includes bibliographical references and index.
Identifiers: LCCN 2017058827| ISBN 9780531126523 (library binding) | ISBN 9780531189030 (pbk.)
Subjects: LCSH: Cuyahoga Valley National Park (Ohio)—Juvenile literature. | Parks—Ohio—Cuyahoga River Valley—Juvenile literature.
Classification: LCC F497.C95 M37 2019 | DDC 977.1/32—dc23
LC record available at https://lccn.loc.gov/2017058827

Produced by Spooky Cheetah Press
Design: Ed LoPresti Graphic Design
Creative Direction: Judith E. Christ for Scholastic Inc.

Published in 2019 by Children's Press, an imprint of Scholastic Inc.

Printed in Heshan, China 62

SCHOLASTIC, CHILDREN'S PRESS, ROOKIE NATIONAL PARKS™, and associated logos are trademarks and/or registered trademarks of Scholastic Inc.

1 2 3 4 5 6 7 8 9 10 R 28   27 26 25 24 23 22 21 20 19

Scholastic, Inc., 557 Broadway, New York, NY 10012.

Table of Contents

Welcome to Cuyahoga Valley National Park!

Cuyahoga (KY-ah-HOE-gah) Valley is in Ohio. It was made a **national park** in 2000. People visit national parks to explore nature and, sometimes, to learn about the past.

In Cuyahoga Valley, there are historic buildings and a **canal**. You will see natural wonders, too.

United States

Ohio →

Cuyahoga Valley
National Park

N
W · E
S

Visitors to Cuyahoga Valley National Park can hike next to huge rock ledges. They can walk through towering trees and flowering fields.

Water plays a big part here. The Cuyahoga River runs through the park. There are noisy waterfalls and quiet ponds to explore.

Hikers along a trail called the Ledges find a stunning view of the valley.

The Cuyahoga Valley Scenic Railroad takes visitors through the park.

Today, mules still pull tourist boats down the canal.

Chapter 1

Life on a Canal

Farmers used to live in the Cuyahoga Valley. It was hard for them to get their crops to markets. To solve this problem, they built a canal. Mules walked along a **towpath** to pull the boats down the canal.

Today, visitors to Cuyahoga Valley National Park can walk along the towpath next to the canal. They can ride bikes there, too. People can learn more about canal boats at the Canal Exploration Center.

The word "Cuyahoga" comes from the Iroquois language. It means "crooked river."

In winter, people can ski or snowshoe along the towpath.

The Towpath Trail is one of five bike trails in the park.

11

Brandywine Falls took millions of years to form.

Beaver Marsh is a quiet spot filled with plant life.

Chapter 2

Natural Sights

There is water everywhere in Cuyahoga! Brandywine Falls is 65 feet (20 meters) high. The falls were carved into the rocks by Brandywine Creek.

The beautiful Beaver **Marsh** used to be a junkyard. Then people in the community cleaned it up.

Many different trees and flowers grow in Cuyahoga.

Violets are one type of wildflower found in the park.

The park has one prairie. This grassland was planted on land that had been a construction pit! Visitors can see violets, bluebells, and many other flowers there. Plants also grow alongside the ponds and streams.

Water lilies grow in Cuyahoga's ponds.

Tall oak, hickory, and maple trees fill the woods in Cuyahoga.

White-tailed deer are a common sight in the park.

Beavers like to nibble on oak wood!

Chapter 3

Wild Things

Cuyahoga Valley National Park is home to hundreds of animal species. River otters glide through the Cuyahoga River. Muskrats and beavers swim in the river and the park's ponds. Raccoons, coyotes, foxes, and deer all live here, too.

Seven different bat species live in the park.

Bird watchers find lots to see in Cuyahoga. Bald eagles and falcons soar overhead. They are on the lookout for smaller animals to eat. Great blue herons nest near the water, where they hunt for fish and frogs.

Reptiles also make their home in the park. Turtles and lizards crawl quietly through the woods and fields.

This is a map turtle. It gets it's name from the lines on its shell.

The great blue heron is the largest wading bird in North America.

All the animals in the park are protected by law. That goes for insects and spiders, too!

The Inn at Brandywine Falls was built in 1848.

Visitors can spend the night at the Inn at Brandywine Falls.

Chapter 4

Visiting the Past

Native Americans were the first settlers in the valley. When Europeans arrived, they built a mill. The mill used waterpower from Brandywine Falls to crush grain to make flour.

These millstones were used for grinding grain.

The settlers also built houses and stores. Today, park visitors can see some of those old buildings.

The Everett Covered Bridge is one of about 125 covered bridges in Ohio.

Visitors to the park can walk through the Everett Covered Bridge. It crosses a creek called Furnace Run. Years ago, covered bridges were built to protect roads from rain and snow.

Cuyahoga Valley Scenic Railroad.

An old-fashioned train takes visitors through the park. People riding on the train experience life as it was long ago. They can also see beautiful scenery.

The park has 125 miles (201 kilometers) of hiking trails.

Imagine you could visit Cuyahoga Valley. What would you do there?

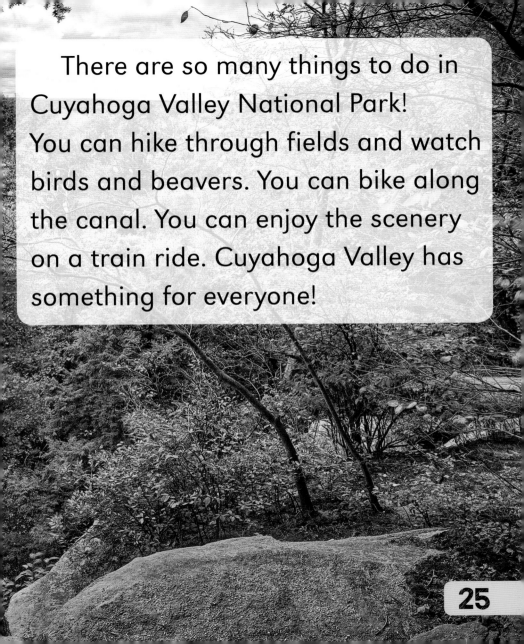

There are so many things to do in Cuyahoga Valley National Park! You can hike through fields and watch birds and beavers. You can bike along the canal. You can enjoy the scenery on a train ride. Cuyahoga Valley has something for everyone!

These are just some of the incredible animals that make their home in Cuyahoga.

beaver

muskrat

raccoon

great blue heron

little brown bat

deer

Wildlife by the Numbers
The park is home to about...

250 types of birds   **39** types of mammals

About 10 species of salamanders live in the park.

skunk

bald eagle

spotted salamander

peregrine falcon

coyote

snapping turtle

43 types of reptiles and amphibians

65 native fish species

Where Is Ranger Red Fox?

Oh no! Ranger Red Fox has lost his way in the park. But you can help. Use the map and the clues below to find him.

1. Ranger Red Fox started at the Ledges in the eastern part of the park.

2. Then he walked west to the Everett Covered Bridge.

3. Next, he headed south to visit his friends in Beaver Marsh.

4. Finally, he took a long ride north to the northern end of the park.

Help!
Can you
find me?

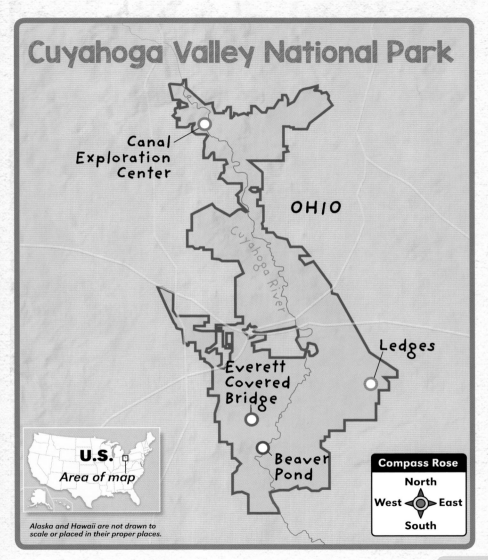

Cuyahoga Valley National Park

Canal Exploration Center

OHIO

Cuyahoga River

Ledges

Everett Covered Bridge

Beaver Pond

U.S.
Area of map

Alaska and Hawaii are not drawn to
scale or placed in their proper places.

Compass Rose
North
West — East
South

Can you guess which leaf belongs to which tree in Cuyahoga? Read the clues to help you.

A.

C.

1. Oak
Clue: Its leaves have rounded "fingers."

2. Maple
Clue: The leaves of this tree turn bright colors in fall.

B.

3. Hickory
Clue: Its leaves are narrow and rounded with a point at the end.

4. Beech
Clue: The leaves of this tree have tiny points all around the edges.

D.

Answers: 1. C; 2. D; 3. A; 4. B

Glossary

canal (kuh-**nal**):
a long waterway built to
connect two bodies of water

marsh (**marsh**):
an area of wet, muddy land

national park (**nash**-uh-nuhl
pahrk): an area where the land
and its animals are protected
by the U.S. government

towpath (**toh** path):
a path beside a canal used
by mules or horses to
pull boats

Index

Facts for Now

Visit this Scholastic Web site for more information
on Cuyahoga Valley National Park:
www.factsfornow.scholastic.com
Enter the keywords **Cuyahoga Valley**

About the Author

Joanne Mattern has written more than 250 books for children.
She likes writing about natural wonders because she loves to
learn about the amazing places on our planet and the animals
and plants that live there. Joanne grew up in New York State and
still lives there with her husband, four children, and several pets.